Thomas Howell

A Few Stray Thoughts upon Shakespeare

a paper read at a meeting of the members of the Clapham Athenaeum, on

Monday, May 30th, 1864

Thomas Howell

A Few Stray Thoughts upon Shakespeare
a paper read at a meeting of the members of the Clapham Athenaeum, on Monday,
May 30th, 1864

ISBN/EAN: 9783337881597

Printed in Europe, USA, Canada, Australia, Japan

Cover: Foto ©Andreas Hilbeck / pixelio.de

More available books at **www.hansebooks.com**

A FEW STRAY THOUGHTS

UPON

SHAKESPEARE.

A PAPER READ AT A MEETING OF THE MEMBERS OF THE

Clapham Athenæum,

ON MONDAY, MAY 30th, 1864.

BY THOMAS HOWELL.

"If a man so highly gifted as to have many sides or phases to his character, and to be able to represent anything or everything in his poetry, were to
come to us, desiring to exhibit himself and his poems, we should do obeisance
to him as a man ; sacred, wondrous, and captivating."

PLATO.

LONDON:

PUBLISHED BY BATTEN AND DAVIES, CLAPHAM. S.

1866.

TO THE READER.

IT was the custom in some of the early Greek colonies for any person who proposed a change in the law to do so, with a bowstring round his neck : in these days any person unknown to fame, who ventures to write about Shakespeare, if not exposed to equal risk, at least is liable to the charge of being rash or intrusive. These pages were prepared for the amusement of a few friends and neighbours, in the midst of important and responsible avocations, and make no pretensions beyond those which the Title-page expresses. The original paper, (somewhat enlarged,) appears in this form, at the suggestion of friends who may have been too partial critics; it is hoped unknown readers will not be less indulgent.

A FEW STRAY THOUGHTS

UPON

Shakespeare.

In the present year, when so much has been written, and well written too, about our great dramatic poet, it will perhaps not be out of place in the proceedings of a Literary Society if I venture this evening to ask the attention of its Members to some observations upon one who has been styled by a learned and profound critic as " the greatest name in our literature, the greatest name in all literature." I do not propose to enquire anything concerning the man Shakespeare—his birth or burial place; the history of his fortunes; the estimation in which he was held by his contemporaries, or by those who lived in the century which followed his death; all subjects of interest, upon which much might be said if we had time for the enquiry; but I will proceed to his writings, and take the volumes now before me— and ask, What do they contain? What do they teach? and I think I shall be able to prove to you that they are worthy of that homage, that universal homage, which men of all degrees and positions of life are so ready to pay. Let us see why it is that

B

great critics, shrewd observers, the most profound
thinkers, able statesmen, the sagest philosophers,
the most religious moralists, aye, and even the keen
worldling, have all recourse to these pages for illustrations of the duties and obligations of life, and
of the various humours, fancies, and emotions of
the human mind. This homage is paid, because
here they find rules for guidance in all great principles of duty, and in that practical action which the
business and incidents of life necessarily demand;
here is stereotyped, by a potent hand, the working
of the human heart, whether excited by the tender
sympathies of affection, distorted by the sinful in-
fluences of corruption, or distressed by overwhelming afflictions of accident or misfortune; we see cases
in which the torments of remorse follow the delusions of crime; we find powerfully displayed the
cheerfulness of the less corrupted heart; the exuber-
ance of good humour, the charm of affection and
kindness, the playfulness of youth, the prattle of
childhood, the garrulity of age, and the truth and
tenderness of love in all its soothing influence upon
the destinies of humanity.

These sources of enjoyment and instruction are
found freely scattered throughout the pages before
us. There must be many here whose hearts will
accompany me in this praise, who have found
unalloyed pleasure in gathering knowledge from
this great teacher, who appears to be an exception

to the ordinary and even the extraordinary instructors of mankind, perhaps none more remarkable. As time advances and knowledge is more diffused, his writings are better known and more widely appreciated. And with each individual man, as life lengthens, the links which bind our affections to Shakespeare grow stronger and stronger. My own experience reminds me, that as a school boy the spirit and action of his scenes commanded my attention, and I was delighted with the humour and mirth which abound in his plays; in after life, like others, I was charmed with the variety and truthful delineation of his characters, the beautiful poetry which enriches every play, if not every page; but as life progresses, and when some objects I once cared for have passed away, I still find the charm unbroken — I now read with reverence the profound philosophy and the unerring wisdom, which he enunciates in language, clear, distinct and expressive; and I receive his teaching with that respect which is due to the writings of a genius, universally admitted to be one of the greatest instructors of mankind.

It has been remarked by Mr. Burke that " no species of writing is so difficult as the dramatic. It requires all the mastery of a complete writer with grace and spirit to support," because in writings of a dramatic character there is little or nothing to influence the mind but what falls from the lips of the personages who appear before the student; the place where every thing occurs is indeed stated, but we have limited descriptions of local scenery, no declarations of the motives which excite, nor reflections upon the consequences which follow the events; no detailed narrative which gives such a charm to the prose writings of our literature. The effect of this characteristic of dramatic writing is shown in an indisposition to study it, the mind requires incident and variety, we like to be told not only what is said, but why it is said, and with what results.

Now in looking at these volumes the first thing which strikes us is the wonderful variety as regards time and place, when and where these scenes are supposed to have occurred; we have the fabulous period of the Trojan War in *Troilus and Cressida*, where the Greeks and Trojans are brought before us with some of the dignity which the student of Homer would expect, but with a large mixture of human follies and human frailties. We have the early history of Rome in *Coriolanus*, where we may see the struggles of democracy and aristocracy in a state devoted to republican policy, the dignified patriotism of a Roman matron, and the chattering gossip of Roman ladies at a morning visit; we see also, with what supercilious contempt a patrician could treat the uncertain and changing passions of the populace. We have another Roman period in *Julius Cæsar*, exhibiting the commonalty of Rome on a great festival, a little of the dignity of Cæsar, the dawn and growth of that great conspiracy which led to his death, the noble-mindedness of Brutus, the passion and jealousy of Cassius, and the faithlessness of Antony. Then we have *Antony and Cleopatra's* history, which Coleridge said was the most wonderful of all the historical plays. These productions are marvellous illustrations of Roman history at the respective periods to which they refer, differing as they did. Ancient English history appears in *Lear* and *Cymbeline*, early Scottish history in *Macbeth*, and Danish history, antecedent to that time when Canute reproved his courtiers on the coast of Dorsetshire, in the play of *Hamlet*, where Shakespeare threw into his work the deep and profound reflections of his own philosophical mind. But Italy, beautiful Italy, "the land of taste and sensibility," calls forth much of our author's genius, especially when dealing with Comedy—Verona, Mantua, Milan, Padua, Naples, and Venice, are places where his scenes are laid in the graceful periods of intellectual development, when the greatest treasures of art and literature were accumulated for the instruction and delight of all after ages; when the freedom of human thought, not a little aided by commerce, induced the merchants of Venice and Genoa to bring the products and riches of the east for the consumption of Europe; and in the grandeur of their maritime greatness, to erect those superb cities which, even in their decay and almost ruin, may be said to live

"In our wonder and astonishment,"

we are called back to the period when the Turks and the Venetians contended for the islands of the Ægean sea; we have scenes in Illyria, Sicily, and Bohemia; a whole play in Vienna; another at Athens; a third at Messina; the blunders of the *Comedy of Errors* take place at Ephesus; *All's well* carries us to the French court; and in *As you like it*, we ramble with delight in the still beautiful forest of the Ardennes. But my list is not exhausted; besides exhibiting the lives and conduct of men and women of all these periods and of all these localities, our poet was a true Englishman. He read with interest the pages of our best historians to good purpose. In *King John*, which has all the beauties of language, and all the richness of the imagination, to relieve the painfulness of the subject, he shows the evils consequent upon power unjustly obtained, and the anguish that treachery and faithlessness sooner or later always bring. Passing by some great periods of English history, he proceeds on to *Richard II.*, and traces his early arrogance, his late humiliation, his sorrow and submission, until his kinsman, the haughty Bolingbroke, takes his throne, and ultimately his life. We witness the gradual decay of *Henry IV.*, under the personal trials to which he was exposed, and the public troubles that constantly surrounded him. *Henry the V.* follows with a great French war, the victories of Harfleur and Agincourt, soon indeed to be reversed in the history of his amiable, pious, but unfortunate son, *Henry VI. Richard III.* next appears before us with wonderful power, and the poet has stamped upon this usurper's name a reputation which in fact is open to some question—some "historic doubts." His English plays conclude with *Henry VIII.* which displays the commanding power and authority of the king; the dignity, pride and fall of Wolsey; the rise of Cranmer; it records the birth of Elizabeth; the sorrows of Katherine, and here we trace the great master's hand in the delineation of the character of the queen. Had the poet left nothing behind him but this perfect display of female excellence, he would have taken a high place in the literature of our land.

From this glance at the times and places when and where Shakespeare's characters existed, I turn to the characters themselves, and here we are lost in wonder at their infinite variety. Kings, queens, cardinals, archbishops, friars, priests, ministers of state, judges, great nobles, courtiers, rebels, soldiers of all ranks, sailors, physicians, merchants, shopkeepers, servants, gardeners, jailers, gravediggers, and, in fact, all classes, all positions of life; but expressly I must note women of all stations, old and young—the dignified Katharine, the noble Portia, the tender-hearted Cordelia, the admired Miranda, the voluptuous Cleopatra, the impassioned Juliet, the joyous Rosalind, and the conscience-stricken Gertrude. These are only a few of his great female characters; many, very many others of equal distinctness, individuality, and grace will at once occur to every reader. In Arthur we have the simplicity of childhood; and the conceits and follies of old age are wonderfully depicted in Justice Shallow. The chivalrous Falconbridge cheers us. The cowardice of Pistol and Parolles amuses. We see with respect the priests and friars of the Christian church always sensible, judicious, and benevolent. We have French doctors and Welsh parsons; mobs and patriots of Rome; the wise men of Greece, its warriors and chiefs. In depicting these varied characters, our author portrays all classes of human intelligence, from the atrocious Iago, the ill-judging Lear, the philosophical Hamlet, or the witty Falstaff,—all intellects of the highest order, down through all the phases of mental power,—to the simplicity of Slender, or the fatuity of Sir Andrew Aguecheek. We have the cynic in Tymon; perhaps a little of it in Jaques; the restless joyousness of life in Mercutio, Sir Toby, and Benedict; and still more so in that wonderful· illustration of wit and humour, Sir John Falstaff. Of servants, what a variety has Shakespeare drawn : the gentle Patience, the faithful Griffiths, the doubtful Lancelot, Juliet's nurse, the dutiful and attentive Lucius, the attached and self-sacrificing Adam. But, in truth, I am here only naming some of the personages Shakespeare has produced. There is hardly any position of life his powerful pen has not touched upon; and in producing a specimen of every class, such as now live and move around us, he has drawn truly from human nature, and exhibits types of humanity for all time.

But boundless as are the varieties of portraiture, reflecting the conditions and incidents of " this our life," this transcendent genius does not confine himself to the realities of our sublunary state, he steps beyond the sphere of human existence,

> " Things of the noblest kind his genius drew,
> And looked through nature at a single view :
> A loose he gave to his unbounded soul,
> And taught new lands to rise, new seas to roll ;
> Call'd into being scenes unknown before,
> And passing nature's bounds, was something more."

and what a subject is before us when we get to the supernatural of Shakespeare. Living in a time of great credulity, when the mind of man luxuriated freely in strange imaginings, he gave to them

> " A local habitation and a name."

He surrendered himself to the inspiration of his muse—she carried him into the wild regions of fancy, and he has coined from the pure metal of his own brain, personalities invested with interest, influence, and often with beauty; the gentle Ariel and the earthly Caliban of the *Tempest* ; the Witches of *Macbeth;* the Ghosts of Hamlet, Banquo, and Cæsar; and beyond all these, the fairy creations of the *Midsummer Night's Dream* — Titania and Oberon, Puck, Peasblossom, Cobweb, Moth and Mustard Seed. What can be more marvellous than these fairy scenes, or more graceful and poetical ? It was left for Shakespeare to embody and fix upon the mind of man the thought and personality of fairy life, which Spencer at an earlier, and Milton at a later date have touched upon.

Having thus glanced at the times and places referred to in Shakespeare's dramas and the various characters embodied by him, we are prepared to go a step further; at present we are only taking a distant view of his writings,—all appears bright, grand, and comprehensive. But our view is still distant and indistinct ; it is not until we come to a nearer examination of the details that we become fully alive to the treasures these volumes contain. When we weigh and measure the words which fall from the lips of the various personages, we begin to appreciate the dignity, grace and beauty which Shakespeare's mind presented; for my own part I believe that could I question any person in this assembly, or every person I met in an hour's walk in our great metropolis, and ask each, What has been your special

care or special joy this day? what do you eagerly
desire? or, using the language of the ship master to
the sleeper of old, "what is thine occupation?"
To each person some words of counsel, or comfort,
reproof or caution, would be found in the pages of our

> " Guide, philosopher, and friend,"

applicable to every case; and these not glancing ·
allusions or far-fetched imaginations, but clear un-
equivocal exhortations of a sound moral tendency,
in words distinct, terse, harmonious, and elegant.

To a young man about to enter upon his travels,
we will give the advice of the Countess of Roussilon
to Bertram, the mother says—

> " Love all, trust a few ;
> Do wrong to none; be able for thine enemy,
> Rather in power than use ; and keep thy friend
> Under thy own life's key. Be checked for silence,
> But never taxed for speech."

Or that of Polonius to Laertes in *Hamlet*, and here
we have the sagacious advice of a man of the world;
here the father says—

> " There,—my blessing with you ;
> And these few precepts in thy memory
> Look thou character. Give thy thoughts no tongue,
> Nor any unproportioned thought his act.
> Be thou familiar, but by no means vulgar.
> The friends thou hast, and their adoption tried,
> Grapple them to thy soul with hooks of steel ;
> But do not dull thy palm with entertainment
> Of each new-hatch'd, unfledged comrade. Beware

Of entrance to a quarrel; but, being in,
Bear it that the opposer may beware of thee.
Give every man thy ear, but few thy voice:
Take each man's censure, but reserve thy judgment.
Costly thy habit as thy purse can buy,
But not expressed in fancy; rich, not gaudy :
For the apparel oft proclaims the man.
Neither a borrower, nor a lender be;
For loan oft loses both itself and friend;
And borrowing dulls the edge of husbandry,
This, above all,—To thine ownself be true;
And it must follow, as the night the day,
Thou can'st not then be false to any man."

Every young man will find these rules for his
conduct in life most deserving of attention. Or, if
we meet another bowed down with affliction at the
loss of a near and dear relative, we will remind him
that "moderate lamentation is the right of the dead,
excessive grief the enemy of the living;" or adopt
the exhortation of the King to Hamlet, shewing
the progress of life, the succession of one generation to another; that death is common to all, and
should be looked for by man.

How solemn is the exhortation :

> "All, that's born, must die,
> Passing through nature to eternity."

> "That the survivor's bound,
> In filial obligation, for some term
> To do obsequious sorrow: but to persevere
> In obstinate condolement, is a course
> Of impious stubbornness; 'tis unmanly grief;
> It shows a will most incorrect to heaven ;

A heart unfortified, or mind impatient;
An understanding simple and unschool'd;
  *   *   *   *
   "Fie! 'tis a fault to heaven,
A fault against the dead, a fault to nature,
To reason most absurd: whose common theme
Is death of fathers, and who still hath cried,
From the first corpse to him that died to-day,
This must be so."

If we meet a man neglecting opportunities which
will never return, and wasting time and talents
which should be employed upon the daily duties of
life, I would tell him—

 " There is a tide in the affairs of men,
 Which taken at the flood, leads on to fortune;
 Omitted, all the voyage of their life
 Is bound in shallows and in miseries;
 On such a full sea are we now afloat,
 And we must take the current as it serves,
 Or lose our ventures."

If we found a man too much engrossed in the
cares of life, he might be told—

 " You have too much respect upon the world;
 They lose it that do buy it with much care."

If we meet one bewailing God's providence, we
should be authorized to say—

   " God is much displeased
 That you take with unthankfulness His doing;
 In common things, 'tis called ungrateful,
 With dull unwillingness to repay a debt
 Which with a bounteous hand was kindly lent;
 Much more to be this opposite with heaven,
 For it requires the royal debt it lent you."

If we meet one who has made a place and a name for himself in the world, we remind him—

> " Honors best thrive
> When rather from our acts we them derive,
> Than our foregoers."

Or to take an illustration from the proceedings of this Society: the last lecture given in this room was from the pen of one of our able Secretaries.* Cotton was his subject; and he told us of the great efforts made to obtain supplies from all parts of the world, to compensate for the deficiency caused by the American war. He spoke, of course, of Egypt, and of the mighty river which runs from south to north, fertilising that interesting country, which, without its aid, would soon become an arid desert. He told us of great works constructed to regulate and extend the irrigation, upon which depends the abundance of the produce of the land. Now we find Shakspeare tells us something of this. Antony says:

> " They take the flow of the Nile
> By certain scales in the pyramid; they know
> By the height, the lowness, or the mean, if dearth
> Or foizon follow: the higher Nilus swells
> The more it promises: as it ebbs, the seedsman
> Upon the slime and ooze scatters his grain,
> And shortly comes the harvest."

And so we might run through the incidents of life, all the cares that weigh upon the human heart, all the humours and passions which stir men's

---

* ARTHUR J. DUMAS, ESQ.

blood to anger, strife, or mutiny, and find something suitable for each. This wonderful variety — this dealing so well and so freely with the passing events around us—these are the qualities which have created such an intense interest in the writings of our great poet.

A Lord Chief Justice, who was subsequently Lord High Chancellor of England,* sought amusement for his leisure hours in tracing through Shakespeare's plays references to the practice and technicalities of the legal profession, and he found them so apt and so frequent, as to lead him to believe "that our author was very familiar with some of the most abstruse proceedings in English jurisprudence," and that in early life Shakespeare must have passed a few years as a clerk in a scrivener's office.

If anything could lead me to adopt the notion that these plays were written by Lord Bacon (of which more hereafter), it would be these legal expressions. I do not mean references to legal practice, which speak of persons and things familiar to all, but to nice technical phrases, used not in the ordinary language of social life, but adopted in the processes of law, and engrafted into the formal proceedings of our national jurisprudence.

A naturalist finds that Shakespeare describes with

* The late LORD CAMPBELL : see his letter to J. P. COLLIER, on Shakespeare's legal acquirements.

propriety the instincts aud habits of many of those
animals which have been created for the nourish-
ment or convenience of man. Where will you find
a better description of what the horse should be ; or
who has pointed out more accurately the qualities
which make up perfection in a dog ? Who has
depicted more truly the daily existence of the honey
bees ? He tells the story of their life with the
exactness of Huber, in his own graceful and poetical
language. The hare, the boar, the lion, the lark,
and the nightingale are all referred to, and many
of their instincts clearly portrayed. The stricken
deer, (and who can read unmoved that affecting
scene in *As You Like It ?*) the swallow, the eagle,
the serpent, and even the glowworm and the snail,
are not unheeded in his lines.

Then the flowers of the field claim and receive
his commendation and remembrance—of trees and
flowers there are descriptions of, or references to, no
less than one hundred and twenty-six different
kinds in his plays—all kinds .of flowers that were
familiar in England in Shakespeare's time are
alluded to in his writings, all natural objects were
especially observed by him, and he notices pecu-
liarities which have escaped even those who wrote
upon the subject. In the *Winter's Tale* he speaks of

> " The daffodils,
> That come before the swallow dares, and take
> The winds of March with beauty ; violets, dim,
> But sweeter than the lids of Juno's eyes,

> Or Cytheria's breath; pale primroses,
> That die unmarried, 'ere they can behold
> Bright Phœbus in his strength."

And what facile use does he make of plants and flowers in the distribution from the basket of poor Ophelia, in the hour of her insanity, when she intrudes unwelcome into the court of Denmark. To Laertes she gives rosemary, saying, "That's for remembrance; pray you, love, remember: and there is pansies, that's for thoughts." To the king she says, "There's fennel for you, and columbines." But to the queen, whose conscience was disturbed, "There's rue for you; and here is some for me." Those who know *Cymbeline*, the *Winter's Tale*, and the *Midsummer Night's Dream*,—and who does not know them?—will trace the poetry of flowers as worked out by Shakespeare, more or less in every play he has produced.*

Of the forests and woods he loved to speak, which might be expected from a Warwickshire man, who learnt in his own beautiful county to

> "Warble his native wood notes wild."

Passages abound in which he gracefully describes the natural incidents of pastoral life; such as

> "The birds chaunt melody on every bush;
> The snake lies rolled in the cheerful sun;
> The green leaves quiver in the cooling wind,
> And make a chequered shadow on the ground."

* Vide Appendix A.

C

Depicting the exiled duke in the forest of Arden, he makes him say—

> "Hath not old custom made this life more sweet
> Than that of painted pomp ? Are not these woods
> More free from peril than the envious court ?
>   *   *   *   *   *   *
> And this our life, exempt from public haunt.
> Finds tongues in trees, books in the running brooks,
> Sermons in stones, and good in everything."

Further, in these pages we find that the Musician also may claim his share in this myriad-minded man. Shakespeare must have been a musician himself, or he must have enjoyed it from his very soul. He denounces

> "The man that hath no music in himself,
> Nor is not moved by concord of sweet sounds,
> As fit for treasons, stratagems, and spoils.
> The motions of his spirit are dull as night,
> And his affections dark as Erebus :
> Let no such man be trusted."

Here, as in everything else, he passes from the most imaginative and fanciful perceptions, to the ordinary incidents of daily life ; " Young Lorenzo " tells Pythagoras's story of the music of the spheres to " Pretty Jessica." The soldiers in *Antony and Cleopatra* hear unearthly and mysterious music, which forebodes the fall of Antony ; whilst Othello is as eager as Mr. Babbage to dismiss the itinerant musicians who play before his door.

His love of the art breaks out on every suitable,

and perhaps on some unsuitable occasions; he alludes to music more or less in nearly every play, and in most unmeasured terms he censures him

> " That has not read so far
> To know the cause why music was ordained:
> Was it not, to refresh the mind of man
> After his studies, or his usual pain ?"

How beautifully does he use it in the *Tempest* where Ferdinand says of Ariel's music,

> " Where should this music be ? i'the air or the earth ?
> It sounds no more: — and sure, it waits upon
> Some God o'the island. Sitting on a bank,
> Weeping again the king my father's wreck,
> This music crept by me upon the waters ;
> Allaying both their fury, and my passion,
> With its sweet air."

Polonius especially desires that Laertes in his travels should not forget to " ply his music." Caliban is not so insensible as to be indifferent to its influence. Cloten attempts to woo Imogen by " assailing her with music;" but although he pronounces it to be " a wonderful sweet air, with admirable rich words to it," she vouchsafes no notice.

> " Hark ! hark ! the lark at heaven's gate sings."

receives more attention in our days, when sung to the charming music written for those words by Sir Henry Bishop. " He hears no music" was one of the reasons why Cæsar loved not Cassius. Henry and Katharine both seek its soothing influence.

c 2

Ophelia sings in her insanity, and Desdemona in her sorrow; even the melancholy Jaques could call for more of it. Sir Toby and his fellows "made the welkin dance indeed, and rouse the night owl in a catch," and the gravedigger in *Hamlet* "sings at grave making" for "custom hath made it in him a matter of easiness." Songs abound throughout his plays; and Matthew Locke, Purcell, Dr. Arne, Webb, Calcott, Stevens, Bishop, and "last, though not least in love," Mendelsohn, have all written charming music to illustrate the poetry of Shakespeare.

Sailors have pointed out the accuracy with which he has detailed their duties in a storm, in the opening scene of the *Tempest*. What can be more admirable than the following manly exhortation, the philosophy of which is applicable to every station of life—

> " Wise men ne'er sit and wail their loss
> But cheerly seek how to redress their harms ;
> What, tho' the mast be now blown overboard,
> The cable broke, the holding anchor lost,
> And half our sailors swallowed in the flood,
> Yet lives our Pilot still. Is't meet that he
> Should leave the helm, and, like a fearful lad
> With tearful eyes, add water to the sea,
> And give more strength to that which hath too much ;
> Whilst in his moan the ship splits on the rocks
> Which industry and courage might have saved."

Soldiers again may, if they please to search for

them, find rules for their daily conduct in his pages; they abound with exhortations to obedience, courage, forbearance, patience, prudence, patriotism, which our own well disciplined soldiers in arduous times always exhibit : nay, more than this, while there are rules for personal action, and unquestionable teachings as to personal duty, there are singular passages which exhibit the general's duty. I found a strange coincidence the other day. In the pages of Shakespeare : Henry V. entering France issues the following orders to his soldiers—

" We give express charge, that, in our marching through the country, there be nothing compelled from the villages, nothing taken but paid for: none of the French upbraided, or abused in disdainful language."

And upon referring to the campaign of the Duke of Wellington, Colonel Gurwood records that, upon entering France the duke issued the following orders the third day after the battle of Waterloo—

" The army is about to enter the French territory ; and France should be treated as a friendly country: nothing shall be taken, by either officers or soldiers, which is not paid for." " The Commissaries of the army will provide for the wants of the troops in the usual manner ; and it is not permitted, either to soldiers or officers, to extort contributions."

He also directed that the people should be treated with respect and kindness. Thus the poet in his closet, who knew what human duty was in all cases, two hundred and fifty years ago; and the great soldier of modern days who always practised it, used almost the same words.

But the doctor, as well as the musician, the soldier, and the lawyer, will find in these pages innumerable references to his own practice. An able writer says on this subject, " I have arrived at the fullest conviction, that our dramatist had at least been a diligent student of all medical know-ledge existing at his time; and he has traced illustrations of this view of the poet's genius exhi-biting a perfect acquaintance with the diagnosis of many diseases, and the results they produce upon the human body when subject to their influence; but (with all my respect and reverence) I am bound to admit his teaching is not always in accordance with the practice of the best physicians. Still there is one class of diseases that flesh is heir to, in which Shakespeare's knowledge was profound : I allude to of course, to diseases of the mind.

> " Canst thou not minister to a mind diseas'd ;
> Pluck from the memory a rooted sorrow ;
> Raze out the written troubles of the brain ;
> And, with some sweet oblivious antidote,
> Cleanse the foul bosom of that perilous stuff
> Which weighs upon the heart."

He who could ask these questions, knew how cruelly the conscience works upon the mind when overbalanced by unrepented crime and guilty remorse; he knew the pressure with which overwhelming sorrow, calamity, or disappointment, disturbed its equanimity, and impaired its springs of healthy energy and action. Many writers on mental diseases refer with admiration to the knowledge Shakespeare displays; of the progress of this most distressing malady they find in his pages the first symptoms of disorder, the various features which signalise its progress, and the terrible events which mark its climax.

Some of our members will remember with satisfaction one, if not two, lectures given to this Society by one of our body,* who was admirably qualified by his professional knowledge, as well as by his perfect acquaintance with Shakespeare's writings, to point out in detail the specialities to which I now refer. But my subject is boundless—we go on from point to point, and all seems yet beyond us; as we advance in climbing a range of lofty hills, one rises beyond another, so we find in the study of Shakespeare's writings that, as we become more and more acquainted with them, they expand. As we ascend, our horizon is enlarged: no practical question too subtle for his pen; no anguish which one of his characters does not reach; no workings of the heart so strange and various as not to be matched in the delineations of life displayed by him. The gentle emotions of love, the gay frivolities and the exuberant fancies of youth, the burthen

* Dr. Dendy.

of sorrow, the haste and fury of passion and anger,
the fierce burnings of unfounded jealousy, the on-
ward leading of criminal ambition ; and, in truth,
every passion, impulse, or anguish, finds palpable
expression, and this, not in a single outburst of
feeling or passionate declaration, but traced from
its earliest influence to full maturity—from the bud
to the bloom—the flower and the decay; and there
is a marvellous consistency preserved throughout :
the character is itself complete—there is an identity
to be traced. Macbeth, who in the midst of an
appalling incident, " dares do all that does become
a man," is the same throughout. Hanging out
the banners on the outward walls, when Birnam
wood has come to Dunsinane, and he is ready to
contend against Macduff, he is the gallant soldier of
the first act :

> " ——— Who carved out his passage
> Amidst the Kernes and Gallowglasses,"

in that war which gave him his sovereign's favour,
and won for him

> " Golden opinions from all sorts of people."

But while this identity of personal character can
be traced in many cases, there is a striking variety
in the different persons influenced by the same
emotions. The misanthropism of Jacques differs
from that of Timon, and both differ from that of

Hamlet. Othello and Leontes are each influenced by the same unfortunate delusions, but they act very differently, and so does Leonatus Posthumous. Henry V. is a gallant, high-spirited soldier; so is Falconbridge, Hotspur, Talbot, and Coriolanus; but nevertheless how distinctly do they vary from each other.

There is another point which deserves to be remarked upon — the appropriateness with which certain nameless characters express themselves. Take the short scene of the three citizens in *Richard III.*, which is never acted; it is so natural, and contains so much wisdom, notwithstanding the censures of Steevens, that I venture to quote it entire. The death of Edward IV. has just occurred, and in one of London's streets these worthies meet; they speak, as some men spoke the other day, when the death of our excellent prince, Albert the Good, took all by surprise, and threw a sadness over the land—a darkness that might be felt. These citizens compare the news they have heard; they bewail the king's untimely death; they are grieved at the succession of the child king; they doubt those to whose care he is committed, with good reason. One more sagacious than the rest throws out cogent thoughts on the prospect before them; and they are so replete with sense and piety that all will find pleasure in their perusal—

" LONDON.   *A Street.*

Enter two Citizens, meeting.

First Cit. Good morrow, Neighbour; whither away so fast?

Sec. Cit. I promise you I scarcely know myself.

　　　　　Hear you the news abroad?

First Cit.　　　　Yes, that the king is dead.

Sec. Cit. Bad news, by'r lady; seldom comes the better:

　　　I fear, I fear, 'twill prove a giddy world.

Enter another Citizen.

Third Cit. Neighbours, God speed!

First Cit.　　　　Give you good morrow, sir.

Third Cit. Doth the news hold of good King Edward's
death?

Sec. Cit. Ay, sir, it is too true; God help the while!

Third Cit. Then, masters, look to see a troublous world.

First Cit. No, no; by God's good grace his son shall reign.

Third Cit. Woe to that land that's governed by a child!

Sec. Cit. In him there is a hope of government;

Which, in his nonage, council under him,

And, in his full and ripen'd years, himself,

No doubt, shall then and till then, govern well.

　First Cit. So stood the state when Henry the Sixth

Was crown'd in Paris, but at nine months old,

　Third Cit. Stood the state so? No, no, good friends, God
wot;

For then this land was famously enriched

With politic grave counsel; then the king

Had virtuous uncles to protect his grace.

　First Cit. Why, so hath this, both by his father and mother.

　Third Cit. Better it were they all came by his father;

Or, by his father, there were none at all;

For emulation now, who shall be nearest,

Will touch us all too near, if God prevent not.

O, full of danger is the Duke of Gloster;

And the queen's sons and brothers haught and proud;
And were they to be ruled, and not to rule,
This sickly land might solace as before.
   First Cit. Come, come, we fear the worst; all will be well.
   Third Cit. When clouds are seen wise men put on their cloaks;
When great leaves fall, then winter is at hand;
When the sun sets, who doth not look for night?
Untimely storms make men expect a dearth.
All may be well; but, if God sort it so,
'Tis more than we deserve, or I expect.
   Sec. Cit. Truly the souls of men are full of fear:
You cannot reason almost with a man
That looks not heavily and full of dread.
   Third Cit. Before the days of change, still is it so:
By a divine instinct men's minds mistrust
Ensuing danger; as, by proof, we see
The waters swell before a boisterous storm.
But leave it all to God. Whither away?
   Sec. Cit. Marry, we were sent for to the justices.
   Third Cit. And so was I; I'll bear you company."

Then the scene of Richard II. and the poor groom has some of the same features. The deposed King is in Pomfret; and shortly before his death a faithful follower finds him out, and tells of the horse that Richard used so oft to ride, and which he had so often groomed. Roan Barbary was used by the proud and haughty Bolingbroke on his coronation day, when he made his triumphal journey through London's streets. Again there is a character in *King John*—James Gurney—he appears but once, and says only four words; and yet Coleridge wrote half a page on this personage, the kindness of

Falconbridge to his old and faithful servant, and the respect and affection of the few words spoken " Good leave, good Philip," are taken by him as a fair illustration of that familiar yet courteous spirit which men of all ranks shewed to each other in the age immediately following the Crusades, when the spirit of chivalry was abroad in the land.

A very short portion of a scene occurs in the *Merry Wives of Windsor*, which has always struck me as being very beautiful. Fenton loves Ann Page, and is loved by her in return; and Ann possesses what in those days was thought to be a good inheritance; as Sir Hugh Evans says " Seven hundred pounds and possibilities is good gifts." Her father wishes her to marry Slender, and her mother, Doctor Caius; both are equally distasteful to sweet Ann Page, and in a short interview with Fenton, she expresses so gracefully and earnestly, her desire that he should " seek her father's love," that I know few passages more admirable; she cannot make up her mind what she will do, if he fails, and breaks off at the point of difficulty; so gently, so tenderly, and so dutifully, that it must impress all readers.

> *Fenton.* I see, I cannot get thy father's love;
> Therefore, no more turn me to him, sweet Nan.
>
> *Anne.* Alas ! how then ?
>
> *Fent.* Why, thou must be thyself.
> He doth object, that I am too great of birth;

And that, my state being gall'd with my expense,
I seek to heal it only by his wealth:
Besides these, other bars he lays before me,—
My riots past, my wild societies;
And tells me, 'tis a thing impossible
I should love thee, but as a property.

 Anne. May be, he tells you true.

 Fent. No, heaven so speed me in my time to come!
Albeit, I will confess, thy father's wealth
Was the first motive that I woo'd thee, Anne:
Yet, wooing thee, I found thee of more value
Than stamps in gold, or sums in sealed bags;
And 'tis the very riches of thyself
That now I aim at.

 Anne.   Gentle master Fenton,
Yet seek my father's love: still seek it, sir:
If opportunity and humblest suit
Cannot attain it, why then—Hark you hither!

"May be he tells you true," how much do these words express.

In the expression of tenderness and especially the tenderness of the female heart; combined with purity and affection, what writer can be compared to Shakespeare, and those who desire to trace this phase of his mind should do so in the graceful pages of Mrs. Jameson.* His characters are literally enchanting; look at the third scene of the fourth act of *Lear*—a discussion between the faithful Kent, and a nameless personage who is called a gentleman; the latter has been sent as a messenger to inform

* See her work on the Characteristics of Women.

Cordelia of her father's sufferings, her sisters' unkindness to the indiscreet and passionate old man. He tells Cordelia of her father's exposure to " the warring winds, and deep dread bolted thunder " on a night, when she says—

> " Mine enemy's dog, that had bitten me,
> Should have stood that night against my fire."

And then when she reads the letter and learns the truth, how exquisite is the feeling with which a devoted and loving daughter dwells on her father's affliction—although assuredly he had not been a kind and good father to her—she rises and shines forth as a bright example of female excellence. There are no violent reproaches at her sisters' conduct. The dialogue proceeds :—

> " *Kent.* Did your letters pierce the queen to any demonstration of grief ?
>
> *Gent.* Ay, sir ; she took them, read them in my presence ;
> And now and then an ample tear trill'd down
> Her delicate cheek : it seem'd, she was a queen
> Over her passion ; who, most rebel-like,
> Sought to be king o'er her.
>
> *Kent.*   O, then it moved her.
>
> *Gent.* Not to a rage : patience and sorrow strove
> Who should express her goodliest. You have seen
> Sunshine and rain at once ; her smiles and tears
> Were like a better day ; those happy smiles,
> That played on her ripe lip, seem'd not to know
> What guests were in her eyes ; which parted thence,
> As pearls from diamonds dropp'd.—In brief,
> Sorrow would be a rarity most belov'd,
> If all could so become it.

Kent.   Made she no verbal question ?
Gent. Faith once or twice she heav'd the name of ' father'
    Pantingly forth, as if it press'd her heart ;
    Cried, sisters ! sisters !—Shame of ladies ! sisters !
    Kent ! father ! sisters !   What ? i'the storm ? i'the night ?
    Let pity not be believed !   Then she shook
    The holy water from her heavenly eyes,
    And clamour-moistened : then away she started
    To deal with grief alone."

Another quality of mind and character can be often traced in Shakespeare's writings, and that is, a graceful appreciation of what is done for us by others.   It is an ennobling principle, and would only be so often found in the writings of a generous and warm-hearted man. ˙Look to Brutus, and see how kindly he treats his boy Lucius ; upon one occasion he calls—

    " What Lucius, ho !   Lucius, I say !
    Would it were my fault to sleep so soundly.
    When, Lucius, when ? awake, I say ! what, Lucius !"

the boy awakes and comes to him : but a little later he calls again.

    " Boy ! Lucius ! fast asleep ?   It is no matter ;
    Enjoy the honey-heavy dew of slumber ;
    Thou hast no figures, nor no fantasies,
    Which busy care draws in the brains of men ;
    Therefore thou sleep'st so sound."

In the incidents which follow the quarrel scene, he insists upon the repose of the attendants ; and he passes a few words with his faithful Lucius which I think you will pardon. Having taken his gown from his attendant, Brutus says,

> " Look, Lucius, here's the book I sought for so ;
> I put it in the pocket of my gown.
> *Luc.* I was sure your lordship did not give it me.
> *Bru.* Bear with me, good boy, I am much forgetful.
> Canst thou hold up thy heavy eyes awhile,
> And touch thy instrument a strain or two ?
> *Luc.* Ay, my lord, an 't please you.
> *Bru.*   It does, my boy.
> I trouble thee too much, but thou art willing.
> *Luc.* It is my duty, sir.
> *Bru.* I should not urge thy duty past thy might ;
> I know young bloods look for a time of rest.
> *Luc.* I have slept, my lord, already.
> *Bru.* It was well done; and thou shalt sleep again ;
> I will not hold thee long : if I do live
> I will be good to thee.''

Again, Queen Katharine—she pleads, in her last letter to the king—

> " My next poor petition
> Is, that his noble grace would have some pity
> Upon my wretched women, that so long
> Have followed both my fortunes faithfully:
> Of which there is not one, I dare avow
> (And now I should not lie), but will deserve,
> For virtue and true beauty of the soul,
> For honesty and decent carriage,
> A right good husband, let him be a noble:
> And sure those men are happy that shall have them.
> The last is, for my men ;—they are the poorest,
> But poverty could never draw them from me ;—

That they may have their wages duly paid them,
And something over to remember me by."

How graceful is the propriety with which she alludes to her women, praising them

" For virtue and true beauty of the soul,
For honesty and decent carriage.''

Also her men—

" They are the poorest,
But poverty could never draw them from me."

Again, in *The Midsummer Night's Dream*, note the reply of Theseus to the Master of the Revels, who tells his prince that the poor players who desire to amuse him with the representation of Pyramus and Thisbe are not suitable for his royal pleasure. Theseus asks, What are they that do play it ? He is answered by Philostrate:

Phil. Hard-handed men that work in Athens here,
Which never labour'd in their minds till now;
And now have toil'd their unbreathed memories
With this same play, against your nuptial.

The. And we will hear it.

Phil.   No, my noble lord ;
It is not for you; I have heard it over,
And it is nothing, nothing in the world ;
Unless you can find sports in their intents,
Extremely stretched and conned with cruel pain,
To do you service.

The.   I will hear that play ;
For never anything can be amiss,
When simpleness and duty tender it."

In all this, and many other similar instances, we see the kindly spirit of the man, and readily understand why Milton spoke of him as " sweetest Shakespeare, fancy's child," and called him "my Shakespeare," and why Ben Jonson terms him, "my beloved master," "my gentle Shakespeare," " sweet swan of Avon," and says, " I loved the man, and do honour his memory, on this side idolatry, as much as any; he was, indeed, honest, and of an open and free nature, worthy, gentle, and beloved." These epithets are confirmed by his writings, and they in return justify the praises of his friends.

But if gentleness shines upon the pages, how profusely does a spirit of mirth and joyfulness sparkle around him. The hand that could now present the contemplative Jaques and the misanthropical Timon, drew also the mirthful Mercutio, the gay and lively Benedict, the gayer and still more lively Beatrice, the loquacious Gratiano, and, above all, the surpassing and inimitable Falstaff, which may indeed be regarded as the *chef d'œuvre* of the creations of our poet's comic genius.

Shakespeare never misses an opportunity of proclaiming the superior qualifications of cheerfulness and good humour; instances might be multiplied. "Frame your mind," says Kit Sly's servant, "to mirth and merriment, which bars a thousand harms, and lengthens life;" and Falstaff urges it as a vice in the cold blooded nature of Prince John of Lancaster that "a man cannot make him laugh."

In addition to what I have said, I must not omit to remind you that Shakespeare was a true patriot. Many passages prove his attachment to his native land; speaking of it, he says—

> "This blessed plot, this earth, this realm, this England,
> This nurse-teeming womb of royal kings;
> Feared by their breed, and famous by their birth;
> Renowned for their deeds as far from home
> (For Christian service and true chivalry)
> As is the sepulchre in stubborn Jewry
> Of the world's ransom, blessed Mary's Son.
> This land of such dear souls, this dear, dear land;
> Dear for her reputation thro' the world."

Again in *King John* is that glorious outburst of true English feeling—

> " This England never did, nor never shall,
> Lie at the proud foot of a conqueror,
> But when it first did help to wound itself.
> Now these her princes are come home again,
> Come the three corners of the world in arms,
> And we shall shock them: nought shall make us rue,
> If England to itself do rest but true."

There are some curiosities of Shakesperian literature, the pursuit of which would be very amusing: Peter the Great did not assume the title of Emperor of Russia until the year A.D. 1721; prior to that date he was the Czar of Muscovy, and yet Shakespeare

makes two of his characters speak of the " Emperor
of Russia." In the *Winter's Tale* Hermione says,

"The Emperor of Russia was my father."

And in *Measure for Measure* the Emperor of Russia
is again referred to. In *Henry VI.* a personage
proposes to produce those who have promised the
Duchess of Gloucester

" To show her highness
A spirit raised from depth of under ground
That shall make answer to such questions
As by your grace shall be propounded him."

Those who have noted the strange incidents of
our own times, will be amused to find that the name
of this person is Hume.

Of late years it has not been unusual for the
authorities, when tracing a criminal offender, to
issue his portrait, with the view of facilitating his
early apprehension, and photography has very ma-
terially assisted the operation. Shakespeare anticipated such a proceeding: in *King Lear*, Glo'ster,
when speaking of his son Edgar's supposed treachery,
says,

" The villain shall not escape,
The duke will grant me that : besides, his picture
I will send far and near, that all the kingdom
May have due note of him."

His constant allusions to the influence of the
moon over the tides was hardly to be expected so long

before Newton taught and established his great philosophy of the universe. The theory of gravitation is almost anticipated in *Troilus and Cressida*, where the faithless Cressida says—but I fear without meaning it:

> " Time, force, and death,
> Do to this body what extremes you can;
> But the strong base and building of my love
> Is as the very centre of the earth,
> Drawing all things to it."

The circulation of the blood, discovered by Harvey and published to the world in A.D. 1619, is almost foretold, when Brutus speaks of the ruddy drops " that visit this sad heart;" and to name one more prescient example, which the scientific discoveries of our own days have almost brought to practical verification, and which is yet so familiar that I hardly like to quote it. The day has almost come when Puck can " put a girdle round the globe in forty minutes."

But the great question has yet to be asked and answered, What upon the whole is the tone and teaching of Shakespeare's writings? Does he extenuate or sanction vice? Does he tolerate what is sinful and unsound? Does he cast any slight upon what is abstractedly right and purely good? Does he teach that fashionable sins may be excused, or that the wealthy or high-stationed may be licensed in indulgence or crime? Does he offer disrespect to the teachers of religion, or disregard to their teaching ? Does he lead us, in fact, in any single instance to depart from the paths of Christian goodness and virtue ? These are not the results of his teaching. His object throughout, and at all times, is—

"To hold, as 'twere, the mirror up to nature; to show virtue her own feature, scorn her own image, and the very age and body of the time his form and pressure."

And no moralist ever taught sounder principles of human duty. It has been truly said, "He contented himself with the simple mission of teaching mankind a cheerful reliance upon the mercy and benevolence of God; to be just and kind to all men; to seek out the *good* in things *evil*, and not after the new philosophy of ferriting out whatever of evil may lurk in things good. He strove to make men wiser and better and therefore happier."*

Had all the precepts laid down by Shakespeare been drawn out as a code of morals and properly arranged under the various phases of human duty, his book would have surpassed the teaching of all moralists of ancient or modern times, for we see how thoroughly he was impregnated from the best sources, how constantly he referred to the instruction which the sacred volume contains; and note the use he made of its practical exhortations, its historical and doctrinal teaching. Several works have been written

* COWDEN CLARKE.

to trace the use Shakespeare has made of holy writ, but I do not think the connections traced are always sound, perhaps a volume written by Dr. Wordsworth, the Bishop of St. Andrew's, and lately published, is the best exposition of these views, but instances abound in which the spirit of biblical instruction occurs, where the letter has not been traced.

But our examination leads us further. I have yet to remark on the copiousnes and richness of Shakespeare's language; I have spoken of him as a moralist and profound illustrator of all the various aspects of human life, but I must remind you how skilfully he dealt with his native tongue, not only did he give to the world thoughts of inestimable value, but he clothed them in language the most captivating and expressive, and here he scatters so much that is beautiful, I hardly know where to go, or rather where not to go, for an illustration. Dr. Johnson said "bring any subject you like from the pen of any author, and I will match it from Shakespeare, and his shall be the most perfect exposition."

> "How sweet the moonlight sleeps upon this bank."

> "But look, the morn in russet mantle clad.
> Walks o'er the dew of yon high eastern hill."

Where will you find such a chain of illustrations as in *King John* ?—

> "To gild refined gold, to paint the lily;
> To throw a perfume on the violet;

> . To smooth the ice, or add another hue
> Unto the rainbow; or with taper light
> To seek the beauteous eye of heaven,
> Is wasteful and ridiculous excess."

How graceful his caution " not to o'erstep the modesty of nature."

What force and appropriateness in his images and in his adjectives " pluck from the memory a rooted sorrow."

> " In the corrupted currents of this world,
> Offences' gilded hand may shove by justice;
> And oft 'tis seen the wicked prize itself
> Buys out the law : but 'tis not so above,
> There is no shuffling, there the action lies
> In its true nature."

Possibly we have seen something to remind us of the truth of this in our own day. You will not expect me to dwell upon such illustrations; it would be endless to do so, every page tells us that Shakespeare had the faculty of uttering what he had to say in fewer words and more expressive phrases than any other writer who ever used our language; hence it is that he has conduced so effectually to secure its permanance. He has, as it were fixed it for all time, stereotyped it for future generations, his words are, to use his own phrase, " Household words." He has left more proverbs, shrewd sayings and aphorisms than any other writer, and the use that is made of him by all classes is surprising.

" Thy wish was father, Harry, to that thought."

" The better part of valour is discretion."

"It is a custom
More honoured in the breach than the observance."

If children in their playful gambols call for
" more sacks on the mill," it is probable there are
adults around them, who do not know they are using
the words of Shakespeare. An arrogant boastful
man, " Out-Herod's Herod." If we wish to throw
a doubt upon a traveller's strange story, we whisper,
" Very like a whale." Very often we hear, " Othello's
occupation's gone," and at other times, " Richard's
himself again." Other familiar proverbial express-
sions will readily occur to all who hear me.
Take a careful and well-written article in any of
our daily papers, Shakespeare's thoughts and
Shakespeare's words will be traced by those who
study him ; while public orators and leading
statesmen freely adopt his philosophical or fanciful
illustrations, all great writers do the same, Walter
Scott, Jeffrey, Macaulay, and Stephen, rarely wrote
an essay on any subject which they did not aptly
illustrate by some reference to our great national
poet ; this has helped to give him the hold he now
possesses on the mind of the world.

In Germany he is perhaps held in greater estimation than in his own country, much as we value
him. I recollect talking with an intelligent German

at Aix-la-Chapelle on the subject of Shakespeare's writings, who told me he had fourteen editions of his works. In Russia he is greatly studied, and of late years France has shown a disposition to honor him. The philosophical Guizot, and the impassioned Victor Hugo, have eulogised this poet and moralist; thus even in the country of Voltaire, and in spite of Voltaire, Shakespeare is now studied and valued. In America they are as enthusiastic on the subject as ourselves; a few years ago I met four American gentlemen at Chester, who had landed the day before at Liverpool, and were at once hastening off to Stratford-upon-Avon, and I felt there were kindred sympathies between us which should not readily be disturbed. Washington Irving's delightful sketch of that place will remind many, of reasons which I doubt not have influenced large numbers of his countrymen and countrywomen too, to visit the fine old church close to the banks of the Avon, with the meadows beyond, where his dust rests in the chancel, in front of the communion table: and when the neighbouring tomb was repaired, the old sexton kept careful watch. Looking into Shakespeare's grave he saw nothing but dust—" I thought it was something to have seen the dust of Shakespeare," says the charming writer who tells the story. It is also something, to see that school where he learnt his " little latin and less greek;" and that humble little tenement, which but for his

great name would long have passed away : and
when you visit the room in which he was born, and
look above, below, and around, and see the walls,
ceiling, and rafters all covered with the names of
men mostly and for ever unknown, you will think
with me, it is an expression of public reverence of
no common kind.   For the future this little cottage
will be preserved; and there is no mansion, castle,
or palace in the land that has so many visitors.

Of late years some strange notion has been
thrown out that these plays were not written by
Shakespeare; he, it is said, had not learning for
these marvellous productions ; they could not have
come from the pen of the young woolstapler, who,
fortunately for the world, was not disposed to
adopt the quiet realities of rural life.   Sir Thomas
Lucy,—whose name I cannot mention without
thinking of the fine old domain of Charlecote, its
ancient gateway and beautiful large entrance hall,
both of which existed in Shakespeare's days; and of
the park and meadows around, with the Avon
running through them; where are some of those
fine old oaks with which Warwickshire abounds,
and which were not saplings three hundred years
ago.   Sir Thomas Lucy obliged him to seek the
metropolis, his necessities in London threw him
into the association of the players, and hence these
works.

But I was referring to the theory that Shake-

speare did not write these plays; and to whom are
they then assigned? To Francis Bacon, Lord Veru-
lam! the founder of the "Inductive Philosophy,"
who changed the thought of the world; a well
trained scholar, one almost born Lord Chancellor
of England; one of the wisest, wittiest, and most
learned of men of all ages—of whom Mr. Burke said,
"Who is there that upon hearing this name does
not instantly recognise everything of genius the
most profound; everything of literature the most
extensive; everything of discovery the most pene-
trating; everything of observation on human life
the most distinguished and refined." With such
qualifications it is difficult to imagine anything
beyond Lord Bacon's powers; but had Lord Bacon
written these pages, our wonder and admiration
would hardly have been less. For my own part, I
have been surprised to see upon what a frail foundation this opinion has been enunciated. I do not
believe it has any basis whatever worth a moment's
thought; but it is strange, it is passing strange,
that Bacon, who lived until the folio of 1623 had
been published to the world, and who must have
seen the plays and read them, should never in his
voluminous and varied productions have referred to
these works or their author. It is also strange
that Lord Bacon, in his "Advancement of Learning," and Shakespeare, in *Troilus and Cressida*,
should both quote Aristotle upon the same point,

and both quote him incorrectly—both making the same mistake; while Bacon, in his address to his peers, certainly quotes from *Romeo and Juliet.* But the evidence of Ben Jonson, the companion and intimate personal friend of Shakespeare, puts the notion out of court.*

When the subject of this paper first passed through my mind, I thought I would conclude it by taking one single play, and tracing it from scene to scene,—not reading it, of course, but detailing the plan and progress of the plot. Do this for yourselves. Take, for instance, *Julius Cæsar;* read it carefully, from end to end; study it; see the progress of the subject, how skilfully it is conducted, what perfect identity is maintained in the characters throughout. You will be ready to fancy yourselves in ancient Rome, upon one of those days when the Roman populace turned out, with as much zeal and earnestness, good nature, and humour, as the people of this great metropolis did, upon a recent occasion, to welcome, not the enslaver of Rome, but that man, who in our day and generation, has done so much to free Italy.†

Perhaps there is one matter still upon which I must say a few words. Shakespeare wrote two hundred and sixty years ago, in an age very dif-

* Vide Appendix B.

† Garibaldi's entrance into London, 11th April, 1864.

ferent to our own, and hence we all find matter
in his pages which modern taste would not sanction, and language which is offensive to the
spirit of these times. It is true he has written
many passages which we would not read to
an intimate friend, and some scenes we should
hardly read a second time to ourselves; but if
there are records of depravity, human nature, I
fear, is not able to maintain an action for libel. Now
we must recollect that in the reigns of Elizabeth
and James there was a freedom of thought, and a
plainness of speech, which, at least as regards the
latter, we do not now permit; all writers of the
period are open to the same objection ; our Rector
would not read one of good old Bishop Latimer's
Sermons from his pulpit, who preached before
Shakespeare's time, or even one of Jeremy Taylor's
who wrote after him, with all his grace, divinity,
and erudition ; therefore I would say to many,
select your edition, you may avoid much that can
be spared without loss ; but for myself and my own
sex, we must learn to choose the good and avoid
the evil; we must take an author as he is; shake
off what is objectionable, "like dew drops from
the lion's mane" ; melt down the ore as it rises,
and if there be, as there most undoubtedly is, a
waste and a refuse, it will only tend to prove the
greater value of that true and more attractive
metal which abounds "unmixed with baser matter."

But we must not overlook the particularity with which even the most trivial things are treated by this gifted man, to whom nothing is too great, nothing is too insignificant.

"Thus has the candle singed the moth."

"Rustling in unpaid for silks."

"Creaking my shoes on the plain masonry."

Many of us here are parents, and we have all been children. Have any present a recollection of the days of childhood, when as a caution, the implement of correction was hung up in the nursery? Our fore-fathers did so, we read.

"Now, as fond fathers,
Having bound up the threat'ning twigs of birch,
Only to stick it in their childrens' sight
For terror, not for use, in time the rod
Becomes more mocked than feared; so our desires,
Dead to infliction, to ourselves are dead;
And liberty plucks justice by the nose :
The baby beats the nurse, and quite athwart
Goes all decorum."

But while our author thus touched upon the trifling incidents of lives, with what vividness does he pourtray certain characters. See the Apothecary in *Romeo and Juliet*, Hotspur's description of a Fop in *Henry IV.*, or Mercutio's of Queen Mab. Jaques's description of all ages, " All the world's a stage," Wolsey's reflections on his departing greatness. What a picture is presented in the descrip-

tion of Cleopatra in her barge on the river Cydnus.
What more dignified than the speech of Brutus,
or more artful than that of Antony, on the death
of Cæsar; or more simple and graceful than
Othello's address to the Senate on having married
Desdemona. These are samples of the might with
which this "choice and master-spirit of his age"
could delineate the incidents of history, or turn
into history the brilliant fictions of his own pro-
ductive imagination.

There is one other point that may be noted,
somewhat in qualification of what was advanced
at the commencement, and that is—not only does
Shakespeare let us know what his characters say,
but he constantly supplies an under current of
thought, as explanatory as the forms of dramatic
dialogue will permit : he drops a few words, but
they tell us "a whole history," and from them we
trace the agitation or anxiety which is carried on
within : thus, in *Henry V.*, after his discussion
with the soldiers as to the responsibility of a king
who leads his subjects to war, in which the soldiers
plead that the king must bear all the sin and all
the blame. What are the first words that drop
from Henry's lips, when left alone? Taking up
the soldier's argument, he says :—

> " Upon the king !—let us our lives, our souls,
>   Our debts, our careful wives,
>   Our children and our sins, lay on the king !
>   We must bear all."

This was the argument of the soldiers, and the king's mind is oppressed with such fearful responsibility. In *Hamlet, Lear, Macbeth*—nay, in all his plays, this thinking aloud occurs, and we are led into the inward working of the soul's emotions, and by a simple expression trace a deeper knowledge of what the poet meant to illustrate, than by pages of diffuse exposition. Those who read these works should attentively note this special peculiarity, and the dramatic skill thus exhibited.

But although I have said little or nothing of Shakespeare's greatest qualities (which I dare not attempt to discuss in this sketch), it is time I should draw this paper to a close, for your patience and my powers of speech are more easily exhausted than our subject. I thank you for your attention; what I have offered calls for great apologies. To those who know Shakespeare well I have only reiterated what must be perfectly familiar; and if there are those who know him not, what I have said will yield but little benefit, assuredly less than I could wish to have conveyed.

Still I shall be repaid, if this humble endeavour encourage any to seek in his pages for a portion of that enjoyment and instruction they have so freely afforded to me; if I lead them to recollect that Shakespeare is for the closet even more than for the stage; and that he is not known by a simple perusal, but only by repeated and careful study. I

E

have necessarily had to pass from point to point, from flower to flower, in this infinite repository of beauties, but I dislike greatly a so-called selection of these beauties. Though sometimes convenient, it is hardly fair to cull choice samples and consider that we have before us the mind of Shakespeare; or to suppose that we have the measure of his wisdom and genius by mere extracted passages, however carefully and judiciously chosen : this seems to me, an attempt to " bound in a nutshell," one who should be regarded " as the king of infinite space." As illustrations of the mind, the genius, the philosophy, or the wisdom of Shakespeare, they are highly valuable; they are thoughts of special power and excellence, gracefully and beautifully expressed; but their real value is greatly enhanced when we find them in their proper place, if they are

> " heaps of pearls,
> Inestimable stones, unvalued jewels,"

undoubtedly they look better in their proper setting: then, this rich philosophy and wise discourse, enter into the doings of life and become of practical utility to us, and those who live and move around us. Thus to night I have endeavoured to select such lines as I have quoted in illustration of the prominent remarks I have ventured upon in reference to the design and execution of Shakespeare's imperishable dramas, trusting that these STRAY

THOUGHTS may lead some of you to make further acquaintance with this great treasure-house of human intelligence; to enter, in fact, if I may be allowed the expression, into the temple of his mind; and if we do this, with study and observation, we shall see the grandeur of the whole edifice; the harmony of its proportions; the gracefulness of its portico; the strength of its foundation; the solidity and durability of its materials : then, and then only, shall we find that the works of our author possess elements of perpetuity: wisdom, goodness, truth, and beauty combined; which will enable them to outlast the Acropolis of Athens, the Temples of Pœstum, the Pyramids of Egypt, and, to disappear only when

"The cloud-capt towers, the gorgeous palaces,
The solemn temples, the great globe itself—
Yea, all which it inherit shall dissolve;
And, like an unsubstantial pageant faded,
Leave not a wrack behind."

APPENDIX,

Note (A.) Page 17.

THOSE who are interested in "the purest of human pleasures," the cultivation of flowers, will find Shakespeare's allusions to flowers carefully traced in "Shakespeare's Garden," by Sidney Brisly; also in "Notes on Wild Flowers," by a lady who is eminently qualified, not only to describe the wild flowers of England, but to trace the various references to them so constantly made by Shakespeare.

Note (B.) Page 45.

THE passages alluded to in the text are as follows:—In the *Advancement of Learning*, published A.D. 1605, Lord Bacon says—

"Is not the opinion of Aristotle worthy to be regarded where he saith, that young men are not fit auditors of moral philosophy?"*

In *Troilus and Cressida*, Act II., Scene 3, Hector says—

> "Not much
> Unlike young men, whom Aristotle thought
> Unfit to hear moral philosophy:"*

* This was said by Aristotle of Political, not Moral Philosophy.

And this play was prepared for the stage, it is thought, in 1609.

In *Romeo and Juliet*, Act V. Scene 3, Romeo says—

> "How oft when men are at the point of death
> Have they been merry ; which their keeper's call
> A lightning before death."

Lord Bacon, in his address to the House of Lords, dated 22nd April, 1621, says—

"Lastly, I assure myself your Lordships have a noble feeling of me, as a member of your own body, and one that in this very session had some taste of your loving affections, which I hope was not a lightning before the death of them, but rather a spark of that grace which now in the conclusion will more appear."

Archbishop Whateley, in his edition of " Bacon's Essays," constantly points out in his notes, words now obsolete, or used only in a different sense, which are to be found in the " Essays " and in Shakespeare's plays. This, of course, was to be expected, as they both lived at the same period ; but there are some very singular coincidences to be traced, a few of which I annex, but the speculation is too curious and interesting to be dealt with in this place :—

Thus, in the *Advancement of Learning* —

> "Poetry is nothing else but feigned history."

Twelfth Night, Act I. Scene 2—

> *Viola.* " 'Tis poetical.
> *Olivia.* It is the more likely to be feigned."

As You Like It, Act III. Scene 7—

> " The truest poetry is the most feigning."

From *Essay on Studies*—

" Some books are to be tasted, others to be swallowed, and some few chewed and digested."

Henry V. Act II. Scene 2.

" How shall we stretch our eyes,
When capital crimes, chewed, swallowed, and digested,
Appear before us."

From *Advancement of Learning*—

" Not unlike to that which amongst the Romans, was expressed in the familiar or household terms of Promus and Condus.

Henry V. Act IV. Scene 3—

" Familiar in their mouths as household words."

BATTEN AND DAVIES, STEAM PRINTERS, CLAPHAM. 5.